ANGRY BIRDS PLAYGROUND

Fun Things To Make and Do

Published by Top That! Publishing plc
Tide Mill Way, Woodbridge,
Suffolk, IP12 1AP, UK
www.topthatpublishing.com
0 2 4 6 8 9 7 5 3 1
Printed and bound in China

ROVIO™
LEARNING

D1077111

CONTENTS

BEFORE YOU BEGIN ...

Unleash your creativity with this Angry Birds' Make and Do Book, featuring your favourite feathered friends and their arch-enemies, the Bad Piggies.

The fantastic thing about all these craft projects is that you don't need many items to make them! Just make sure you've got card, glue, paint, paintbrushes, scissors and tape, then gather together a collection of materials that are heading for the bin! Once you have a treasure trove of cartons and containers, you are well on the way to hours of fun making an endless array of brilliant Angry Birds' models and craft activities!

By following the step-by-step instructions in this book, you will soon be transforming everyday items into fantastic Angry Birds' crafts to show to all of your friends. So what are you waiting for? Get crafting!

MINION SKITTLES

Dish out revenge on the pesky Pigs by bowling them over! Challenge your friends to see who can get the highest score by knocking over these Bad Piggies — then stand them back up and try again! It's as much fun making the skittles as playing the game, so collect as many bottles as you can for maximum pig-poppin' action.

You will need:
- One balloon
- Newspaper
- Wallpaper paste
- String
- Paint and paintbrushes
- White paper
- Six plastic bottles with lids
- Thin card
- Scissors
- A black marker pen
- Strong PVA glue

1 Inflate a round balloon until it is about 10 cm (4 in.) across. Tear a newspaper into 2.5 cm x 2.5 cm (1 in. x 1 in.) squares. Mix the paper with wallpaper paste and cover the balloon with a couple of layers of papier mâché.

2 Tie a piece of string around the neck of the balloon, as shown, and hang it somewhere warm to dry. Then add more layers of papier mâché, allowing them to dry in between, until you have about seven or eight layers.

3 Once the papier mâché is dry, pop the balloon and remove it. Paint the ball red, then trace the Red Bird features on page 11 onto a piece of paper. Paint the features, then cut them out and stick them to the ball.

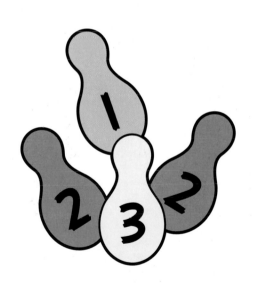

4 Pour a little paint (any colour) into each of the bottles and tightly screw on the lid. Shake the bottle until the paint completely covers the inside.

5 Copy the skittle template (p.6) onto thin card, then paint them to match the bottles. You can make the game more exciting by giving scores to each coloured skittle.

6 Trace the Minions (p.6) onto thin card. Paint them green and leave to dry. Then use a black marker to draw on facial features. Finally, glue the Minions to the skittle templates, before gluing to the bottles.

MINION SKITTLE TEMPLATES

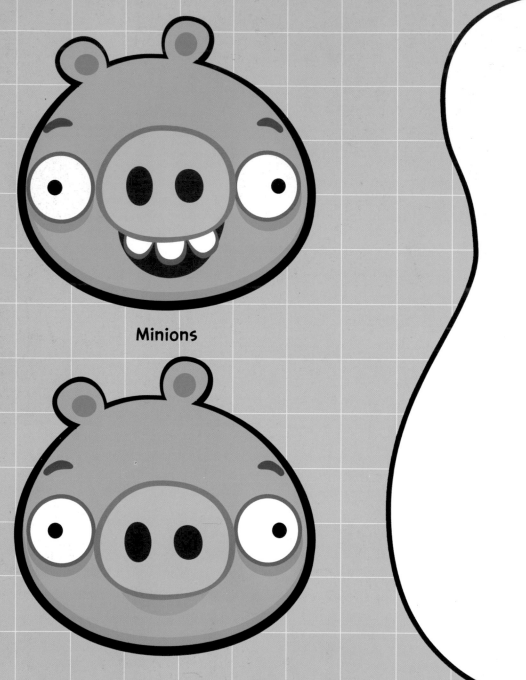

Minions

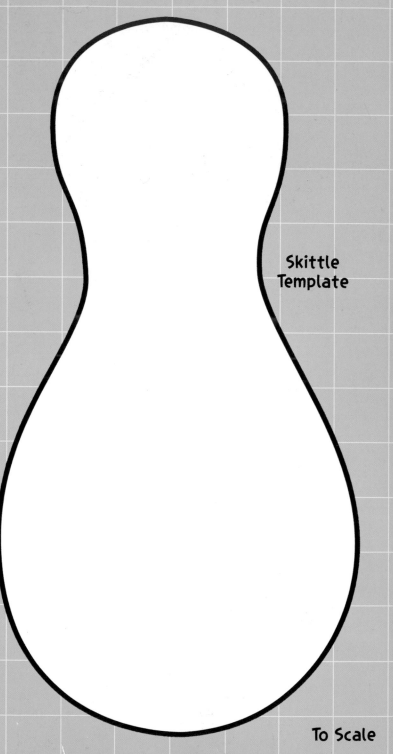

Skittle
Template

To Scale

6

ANGRY BIRDS' TOTEM POLE

Use this fun totem pole to store your favourite pens, pencils, rubbers ... whatever you like! Red, Chuck and Jake will keep them safe from any Bad Piggies!

You will need:
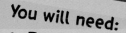
- *Three small round crisp cartons (two with lids)*
- *Scissors*
- *Red, blue and yellow paper*
- *Strong PVA glue*
- *A black marker pen*
- *Thin white card*
- *Felt-tip pens*

1 Glue a strip of coloured paper around each of the cartons, as shown. Make one red, one yellow and one blue.

2 Add detail to the top and bottom of each carton using a black marker pen.

3 Glue each tail to its matching carton, as shown. Scale up and trace the templates on pages 10-11, then colour them in and add detail.

4 Glue each bird's face to its matching carton, using the picture opposite as a guide.

5 Apply glue to the front of the tab on Chuck's Crest and stick it inside the top carton, as shown.

6 Glue the base to the bottom of the red carton.

7 Stack the cartons on top of one another, as shown.

You could keep your pens at the top and store your rubbers, sharpeners and keepsakes in the two bottom sections.

ANGRY BIRDS' TOTEM POLE TEMPLATES

Scaling Up
The term 'scale up' is referred to when you need to draw up the templates. This just means drawn up bigger than they appear on the page.

All the squares on the template page are equal to a 25 mm (1 in.) measurement, although on the page they appear smaller. So you need to draw up a grid of squares that measure 25 mm (1 in.) on all sides, onto a piece of card. Then, using a pencil and ruler, carefully copy what you see on the template page into each square of your grid.

Chuck's
Crest

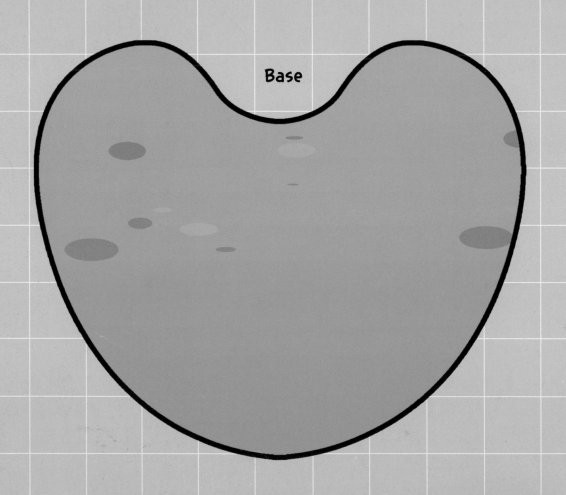

Base

Chuck's Tail

Jake's Tail

Red's Tail

Chuck

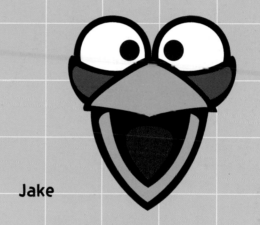

Jake

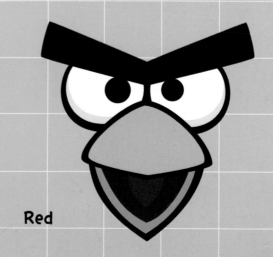

Red

Red Bird Sock Puppet

Very quick and easy to make, this Red Bird sock puppet will soon have any Bad Piggies abandoning their mission!

You will need:

- A black marker pen
- Two ping pong balls
- Thin white card
- Scissors
- Paint
- Paintbrushes
- Strong PVA glue
- A red sock

1 Use a black marker pen to draw pupils onto the two ping pong balls.

2 Trace the templates (pp.14-15) onto thin white card and carefully cut them out. Paint each piece and then leave to dry.

3 Glue the ping pong balls and eyebrows to the face. Slide the sock onto your hand, then put your fingers through the hole and form a mouth shape, as shown.

4 Fold the two parts of the beak down the centre. Glue the top and bottom beak pieces to the sock, as shown. This completes your Red Bird Sock Puppet.

13

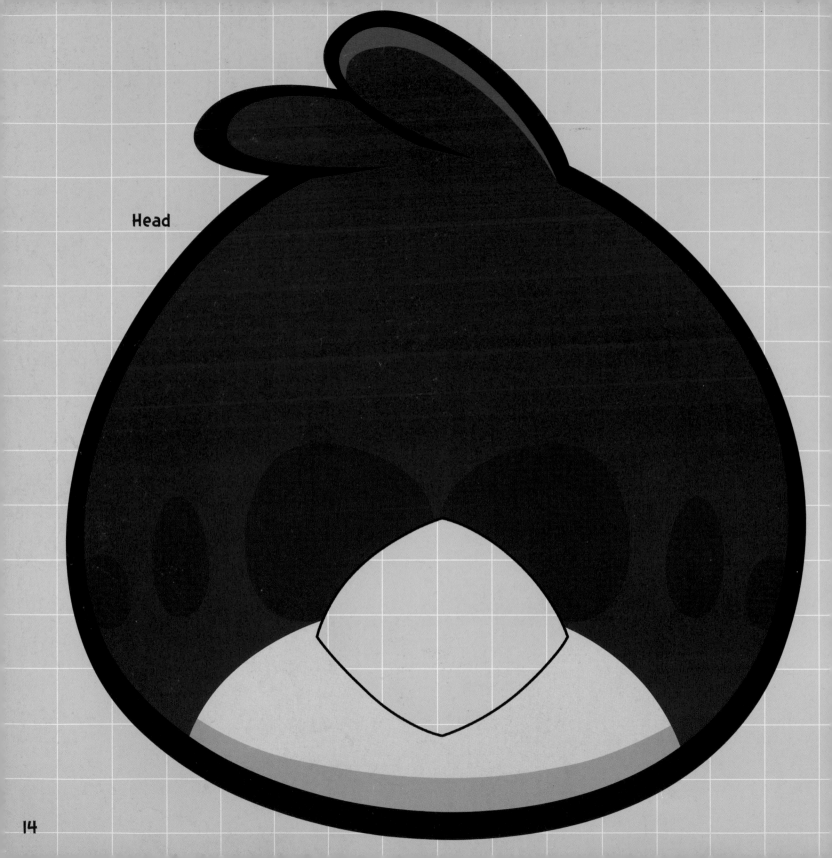

Head

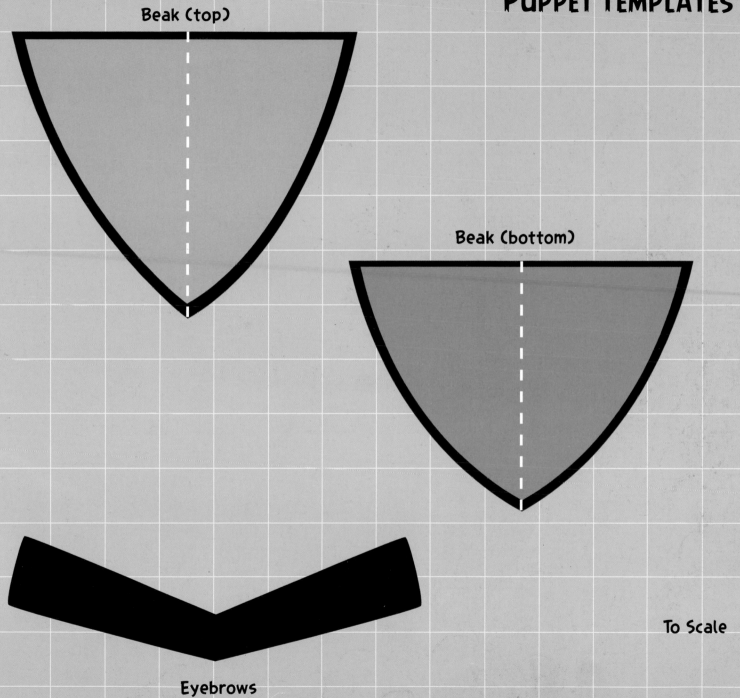

Beak (top)

Beak (bottom)

Eyebrows

To Scale

Red Bird's Paper Plane

Red Bird's plane has been designed to perform acrobatic loop the loops. Try launching Red from a hilltop or on a windy beach and watch him fly!

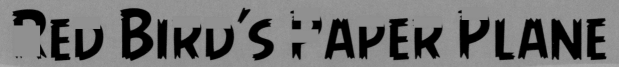

You will need:

- A sheet of red paper (160 mm x 230 mm / 6¼ in. x 9 in.)
- Sticky tape
- White paper
- Colouring pens
- Scissors
- Glue

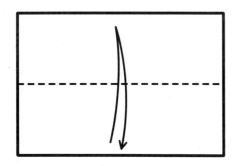

1 Fold and unfold the red paper in half lengthways.

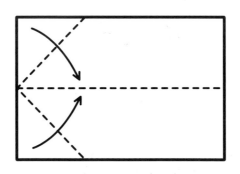

2 Fold the left-hand corners over to meet the middle fold line.

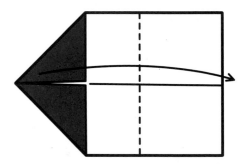

3 Fold the left-hand point over so that it overlaps the right-hand side.

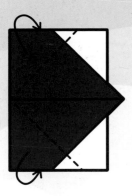  

4 Fold the left-hand corners behind to meet the middle fold-line.

5 Fold the left-hand point over to meet the right-hand edge.

6 Fold the bottom edge behind to meet the top edge.

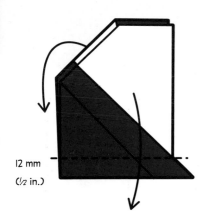 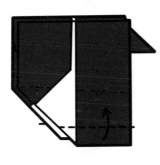 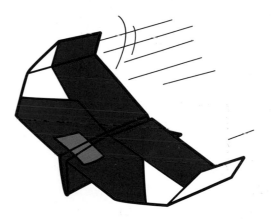

12 mm
(½ in.)

7 Fold the front flap forwards and the back flap behind, making the wings.

8 Fold over a little of the front wing's bottom edge. Repeat on the back wing.

9 Open out the wings, as shown. Hold the wings together with a piece of sticky tape. On white paper, draw and colour in Red Bird, then cut out in a circle. Glue Red to each wing to finish.

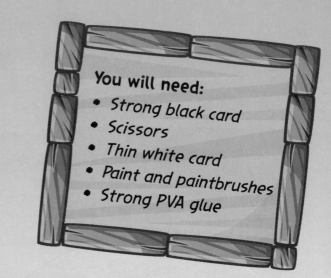

You will need:
- Strong black card
- Scissors
- Thin white card
- Paint and paintbrushes
- Strong PVA glue

BOMB'S MONEY BOX

Nobody will dare to go near your savings with Bomb on the lookout!

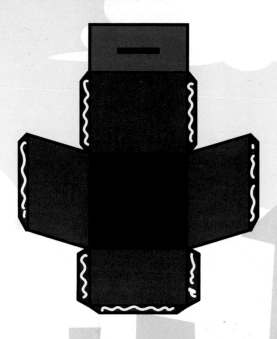

1 Copy and scale up the box template on pages 20-21 onto black card and cut it out. Ask an adult to score along the white dotted lines, as described on page 20, if you are using thick card.

2 Ask an adult to cut out the slot at the top of the box. Apply glue to the tabs, as shown, and fold up the box. Leave to dry.

3 Trace Bomb's features (p.20) onto thin white card. Cut them out and paint on his facial features. Glue to the front of the box.

4 Fold the tab on the crest forwards and apply glue to the back of the tab. Stick it to the top of the box, as shown, to complete your money box.

BOMB'S MONEY BOX TEMPLATES

If you are using thick card, scoring along the white dotted lines will make the box easier to fold. Using a ruler as a guide, ask an adult to gently run the blunt side of a scissor blade along the lines.

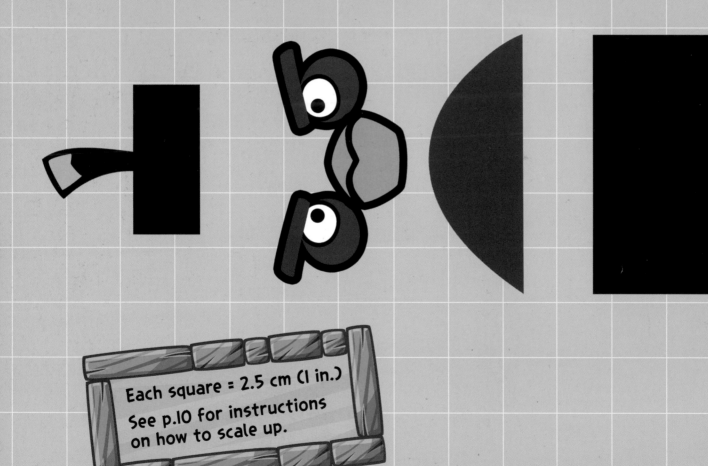

Each square = 2.5 cm (1 in.)

See p.10 for instructions on how to scale up.

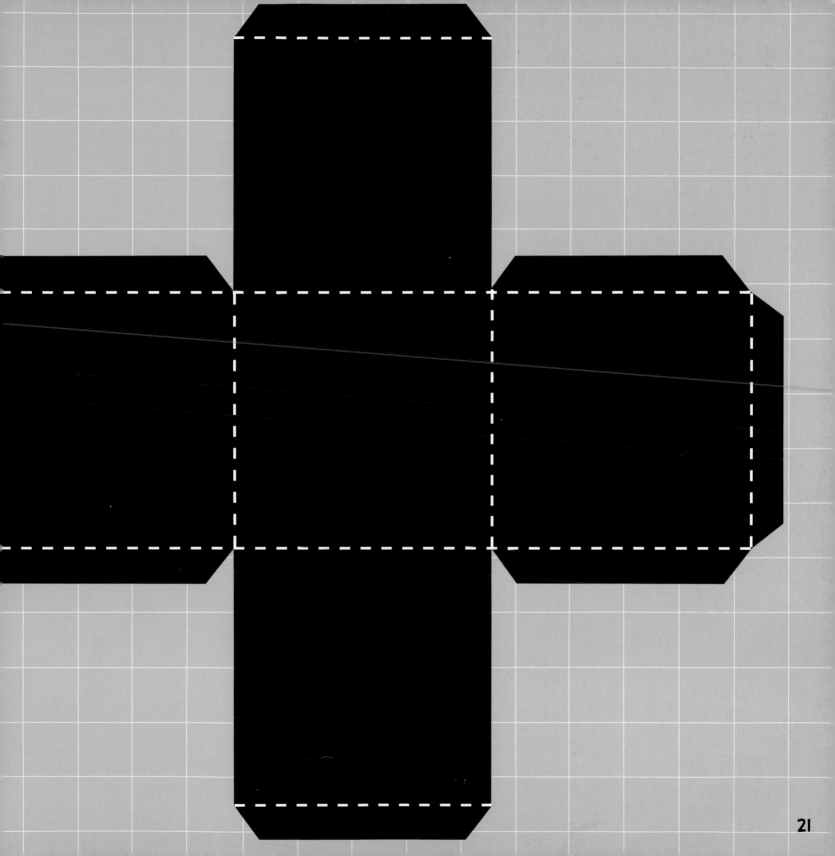

Papier Mâché Piggy

Papier mâché is fun and easy to make, so why not create a whole army of Bad Piggies?

1 Cut lots of strips of newspaper into 2 cm (³/₄ in.) squares. These are used to cover your balloon. Make sure you prepare plenty of strips before you begin as your hands might get a bit sticky. Next, ask an adult to make up 500 ml (1 pint) of wallpaper paste. Mix well and store in a resealable container.

2 Blow a balloon up to about 12 cm (4 ³/₄ in.) in length. Mix the wallpaper paste with the paper. When it is soft, cover the balloon with two or three layers and allow to dry. Apply more layers, allowing them to dry in between, until you have about seven. You can stick the balloon to your work surface with some sticky putty to keep it steady.

3 Tie a piece of string around the knotted end of the balloon and hang it up to dry completely.

4 While the balloon is drying, roll up a ball of papier mâché and squash it to make a nose shape. Then cut a circle of card about 15 cm (6 in.) in diameter for the base and paint it.

5 Burst the balloon and remove it. Ask an adult to carefully cut around the bottom of the head so that it sits on the base without wobbling. Stick the head to the base.

6 Use papier mâché to stick the nose onto the face, as shown.

7 Paint the head and nose green and leave to dry. Copy the templates (p.25) onto thin white card. Paint or draw on the details and cut them out.

8 Glue the ears, eyes and nose onto the face, as shown. Paint or draw on the eyebrows to finish.

PAPIER MÂCHÉ MATILDA

Follow the steps to make Matilda to challenge the Bad Piggies!

1   Follow instructions 1–5 on pages 22–23 (but don't make a nose). Paint the head white.

2   Copy the templates (p.25) onto thin white card. Paint or draw on the details and cut them out. Glue the crest and tail onto Matilda.

3   Complete Matilda by sticking on the eyes, eyebrows and beak.

To Scale

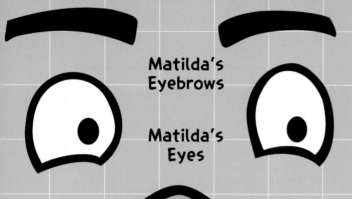

Matilda's
Eyebrows

Matilda's
Eyes

Minion Ears

Minion
Eyes

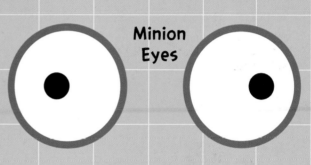

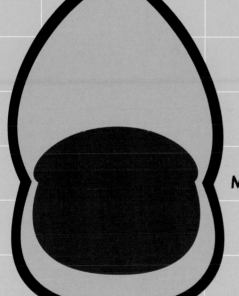

Matilda's Beak

Matilda's
Tail

Matilda's
Crest

Minion Nose

25

ANGRY BIRDS' BISCUITS

Once you've mastered these tasty Red Bird biscuits, you could experiment with other shapes, using the templates in this book.

Equipment you will need:

- Greaseproof paper
- Thin card
- Scissors
- Mixing spoon
- Mixing bowl
- Rolling pin
- Knife
- Baking tray
- Wire rack

Ingredients you will need:

- 125 g (4 ½ oz) butter
- 100 g (4 oz) caster sugar
- 75 g (3 oz) brown sugar
- 1 egg
- A few drops of vanilla extract
- 150 g (5 oz) plain flour
- ½ teaspoon baking powder
- 50 g chocolate chips

1 Trace Red Bird, above, onto a piece of card. Cut it out – this will be a template for your biscuits.

2 Ensure the butter is soft by leaving it out of the fridge for about an hour at room temperature. Then place it in a mixing bowl and mix in both sugars. Beat well. Then add the egg and vanilla extract. Beat well.

3 Now sift in the flour and baking powder. Stir into the mixture, then add the chocolate chips.

4 Using a rolling pin, roll out the dough to a thickness of about 1-2 cm ($^1/_4$-$^3/_4$ in.).

5 Using the template and a knife, ask an adult to help you cut as many Red Bird shapes from the dough as you can. Place the biscuits onto greaseproof paper on a baking tray.

6 Ask an adult to put the tray in a preheated oven (180°C/ 350°F/ gas mark 4) for 15 - 20 minutes or until golden brown. Ask an adult to remove the biscuits from the oven and transfer them to a wire rack to cool.

CHUCK'S JET-PROPELLED RACER

Use vinegar, water and baking powder to propel Chuck forwards on his amazing racer!

You will need:
- Thick and thin card
- Scissors
- Sticky putty
- Two pencils
- Small, empty plastic bottle
- Sticky tape
- Paints and paintbrushes
- Water
- Vinegar
- Baking powder
- A tissue
- Cork

1 Trace the wheels (p.30) onto thick card four times, then cut them out. Make a hole in the middle of each circle by placing them, one at a time, on top of the sticky putty and pushing the sharpened end of a pencil through the centre.

2 Put one wheel on each end of the pencils to make two axles. Stick the axles to the bottom of the bottle with sticky tape, as shown.

3 Trace the two Chuck templates (p.30) onto thin card then cut them out. Paint on Chuck's features. Stick the two templates together, back to back, without applying glue to the white tabs. Open up the tabs and glue them to the bottle, as shown.

4 Put one half cup each of water and vinegar into the bottle. Put one heaped teaspoon of baking powder in the middle of the tissue; pull up the edges and twist the top so the baking powder cannot escape.

5 Take your bottle outside. Drop the tissue and baking powder into the bottle and push the cork into the top. Place the bottle on its wheels, then stand back and wait.

6 The gas will gradually build up inside the bottle and the cork will shoot off, propelling the bottle forwards.

Chuck's Jet-Propelled Racer Templates

To Scale

Wheels

Chuck

POMPOM PIGGIES

Attach your pompom piggies to
pieces of elastic and watch them fly.

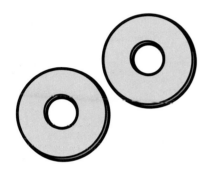

1 Copy the pompom templates
(p.33) onto a piece of cereal box
cardboard. Carefully cut them both
out and place together.

2 Wind up a ball of wool until it will
just squeeze through the hole in the
middle of your pompom templates.
Knot one end of the wool around the
two templates, as shown.

3 Carefully wind the wool around the
ring, as shown. Keep going until
you have completely covered the
templates with wool.

4 If you run out of wool before you
have filled the hole in the ring, wind up
another small ball of wool and knot the
two ends together close to the centre,
where the knot will not be seen.

5 Carry on winding the wool
around the ring until the hole in
the middle disappears. Now tie
the end of the wool so that it
will not come undone.

6 Take a pair of scissors and carefully snip through the layers of wool until you find the edges of the two cardboard templates. Pull these templates apart so that you can get your scissors in between them and then cut all the way around them, as shown. You may need some help from an adult.

7 Take a length of wool and slip it in between the two cardboard templates. Pull it tight and tie it in a knot so it holds all of the wool together. Now trim off the ends of the length of wool and carefully cut off the two templates.

8 Sew a piece of elastic to the centre of your pompom.

9 Copy the Minion features opposite onto thin white card. Paint or colour in the features and then glue them to your pompom.

POMPOM PIGGIES TEMPLATES

Minion Face

Pompom Templates

Minion Ears

To Scale

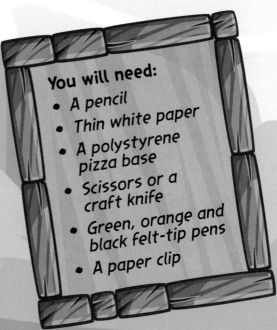

You will need:
- A pencil
- Thin white paper
- A polystyrene pizza base
- Scissors or a craft knife
- Green, orange and black felt-tip pens
- A paper clip

HAL'S PIZZA BASE FLIER

Pizza packaging provides some real airborne antics with this fantastic flier. Instead of throwing away the base after polishing off a tasty pizza, transform it into a swooping Hal. It's quick and simple to make, and you can work up an appetite for your next pizza by taking it for a spin!

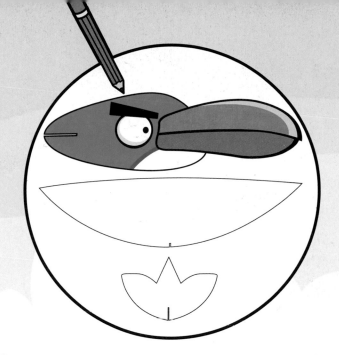

1 Trace the templates (p.37) onto a piece of paper and cut them out.

2 Lay the three templates onto the polystyrene pizza base and carefully draw around them. You should be able to get all three pieces out of one base.

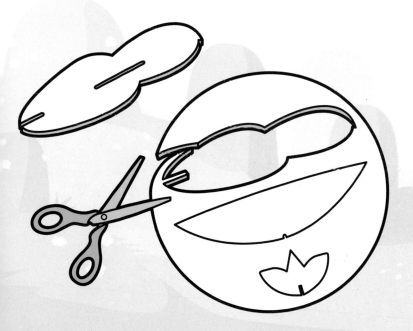

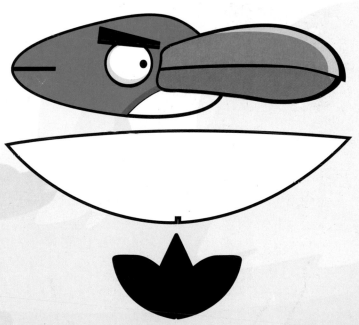

3 Ask an adult to help you cut out the parts. Using scissors or a craft knife, make the slots in each piece (see p.37). Each slot should be approx. 3 mm (1/8 in.) in depth.

4 Using felt-tip pens, colour in Hal's body and tail, as shown.

5 Push the wings through the large slot cut in the body, as shown.

6 Push the tail through the small slot cut in the back of the body, as shown.

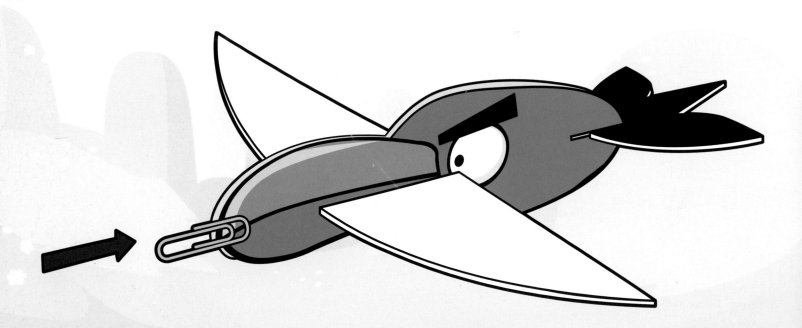

7 Add a large paper clip to the front of your flier, as shown. This will help it to fly further. Then, throw it in the air and watch Hal fly!

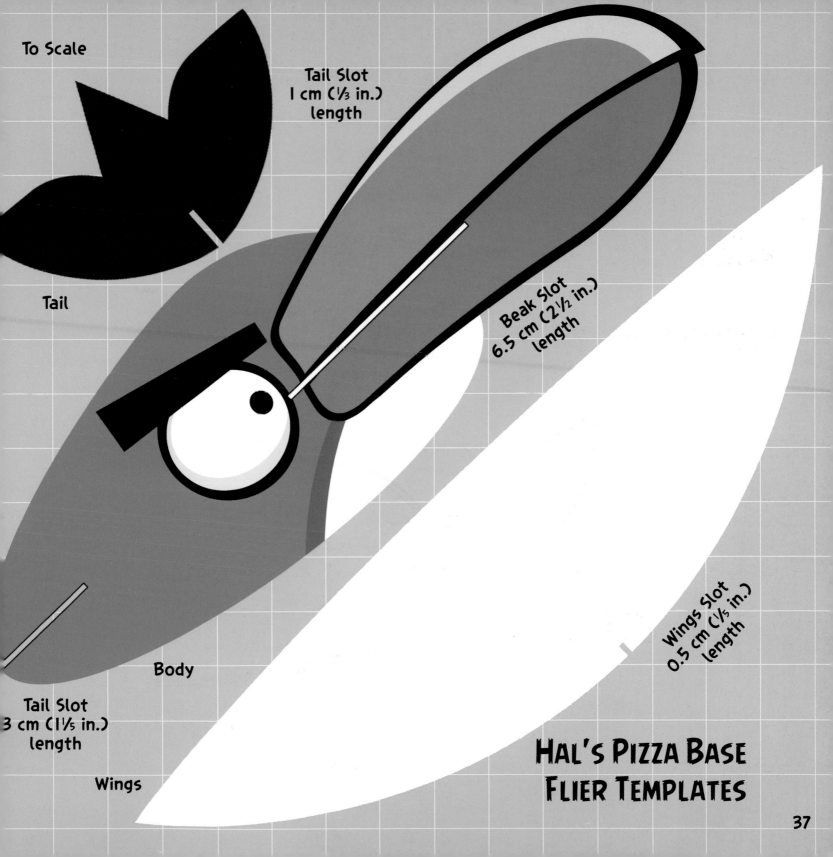

To Scale

Tail Slot
1 cm (⅓ in.)
length

Tail

Beak Slot
6.5 cm (2½ in.)
length

Wings Slot
0.5 cm (⅕ in.)
length

Body

Tail Slot
3 cm (1⅕ in.)
length

Wings

**HAL'S PIZZA BASE
FLIER TEMPLATES**

CHUCK'S TUMBLING LEAF

Chuck is always catapulting himself into trees! Luckily he knows how to use a falling leaf to get back down!

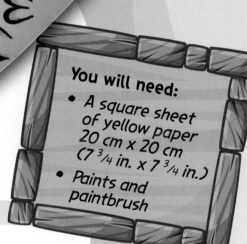

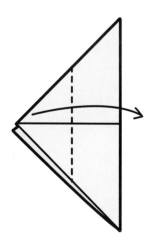

You will need:
- A square sheet of yellow paper 20 cm x 20 cm (7 3/4 in. x 7 3/4 in.)
- Paints and paintbrush

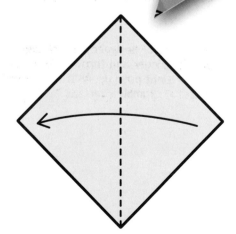

1 Fold the square of yellow paper in half to form a triangle, as shown.

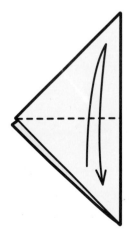

2 Fold the triangle in half from bottom to top, then unfold again.

3 Fold the left-hand point over so that it overlaps the right-hand side.

 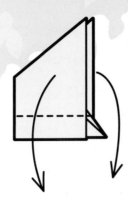 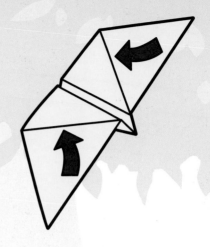

4 Now fold in half from bottom to top.

5 Fold the front flap forwards and the back flap behind, to form the wings.

6 Lift the wings up so that they are horizontal. Open them out a little, as shown.

7 Use paints to add Chuck to the centre triangle of the flier, as shown opposite. Then paint lots of leaves to cover up the wings. Leave to dry.

8 Hold the leaf between your thumb and forefinger and throw it forwards with a slight push up. As it falls, it will gracefully tumble over and over.

39

ANGRY BIRDS' STATIONERY

You'll be the envy of all your friends with this super cool Angry Birds' stationery!

You will need:

- White card
- Scissors or a craft knife
- Fine black marker pen
- Stationery
- Paints and paintbrush, or felt-tip pens
- Acrylic paint if painting on PVC stationery

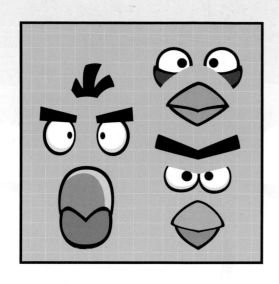

1 Trace the features on page 42 onto white card.

2 Ask an adult to cut out the shapes using scissors or a craft knife. This will make a stencil sheet.

3 Using a black marker pen, carefully draw around the stencils onto your stationery.

4 Once you have transferred the outlines onto the stationery, colour in or paint the designs and leave to dry.

ANGRY BIRDS' STATIONERY TEMPLATES

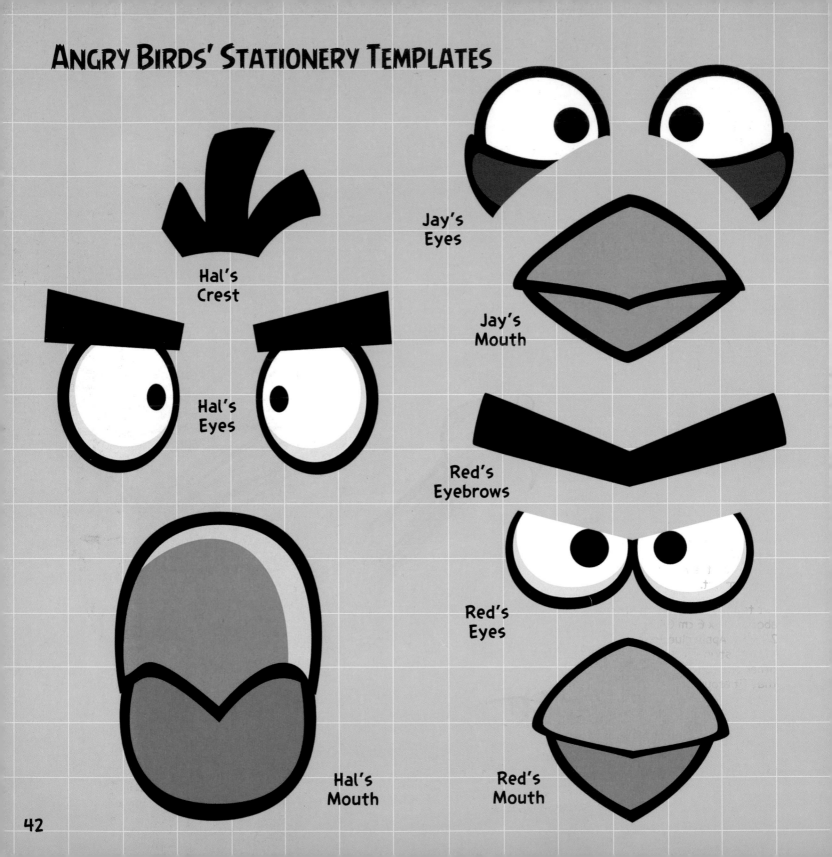

Hal's Crest

Jay's Eyes

Jay's Mouth

Hal's Eyes

Red's Eyebrows

Hal's Mouth

Red's Eyes

Red's Mouth

FINGER 'FOWL' PLAY

Copy these characters to create an Angry Birds' flock. Then arm a friend with a handful of Bad Piggies and start the action!

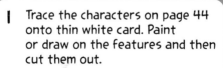

You will need:
- Thin white card
- Scissors or a craft knife
- Paints and paintbrush, or felt-tip pens
- Glue

1. Trace the characters on page 44 onto thin white card. Paint or draw on the features and then cut them out.

2. Cut ten strips of card measuring about 1 cm x 6 cm (⅟₂ in. x 2 ½ in.). Apply glue to one end of each strip and stick it to the other end to form ten rings that fit around the tips of your fingers.

3. Glue your favourite characters' heads to each ring of card. Put the rings on and let the games begin!

FINGER 'FOWL' PLAY TEMPLATES

To Scale

Red

Chuck

Bomb

The Blues

Minion Pig

Hal

Foreman Pig

Terence

The Blues

King Pig

Bubbles

Corporal Pig

Minion Pig

Matilda

Chuck

Bomb

44

KING PIG'S CROWN

Get ready to rule the roost
with King Pig's golden crown.

You will need:
- Thin white card
- Paints and paintbrush
- Scissors
- Glue
- Elastic

1 Trace King Pig's crown (pp.46-47) onto thin white card. Paint the crown using yellow, orange and blue paint. Once dry, cut it out.

2 Bend the crown around, glue the tab to the inside of the other end and leave to dry.

3 Ask an adult to make holes on each side of the crown, as indicated. Thread the elastic through the holes and adjust the length to fit under your chin. Then tie a knot at both ends to secure.

King Pig's Crown Template

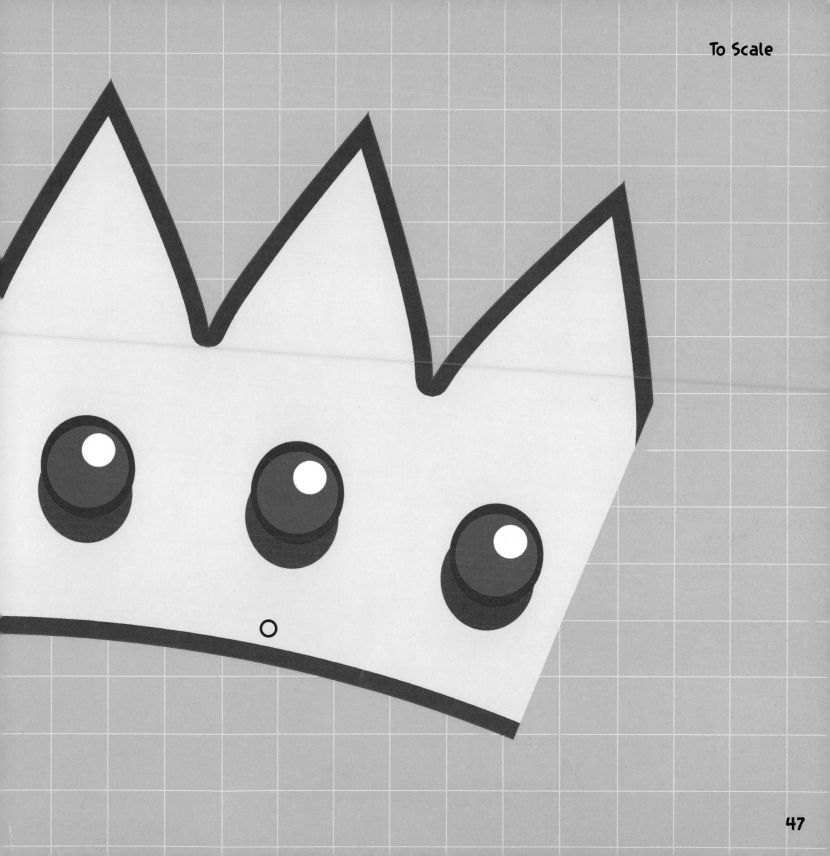

Red Bird Balloon

Transform a boring balloon into brilliant Red Bird.

You will need:

- White card
- Paints and paintbrush, or felt-tip pens
- Scissors
- A red balloon
- Glue

1 Trace the templates on page 49 onto white card. Colour in or paint the pieces to match the templates, then cut them out.

2 Blow up the red balloon and tie off. Glue on Red's eyes, eyebrows and mouth, as shown.

3 Apply glue to the two halves of the tail, but not the red tabs. Stick the two halves of the tail together, back to back. Fold the red tabs outwards and glue them to the back of the balloon.

4 Fold the tab of Red's crest forwards. Glue the crest's tab to the top of the balloon to finish.

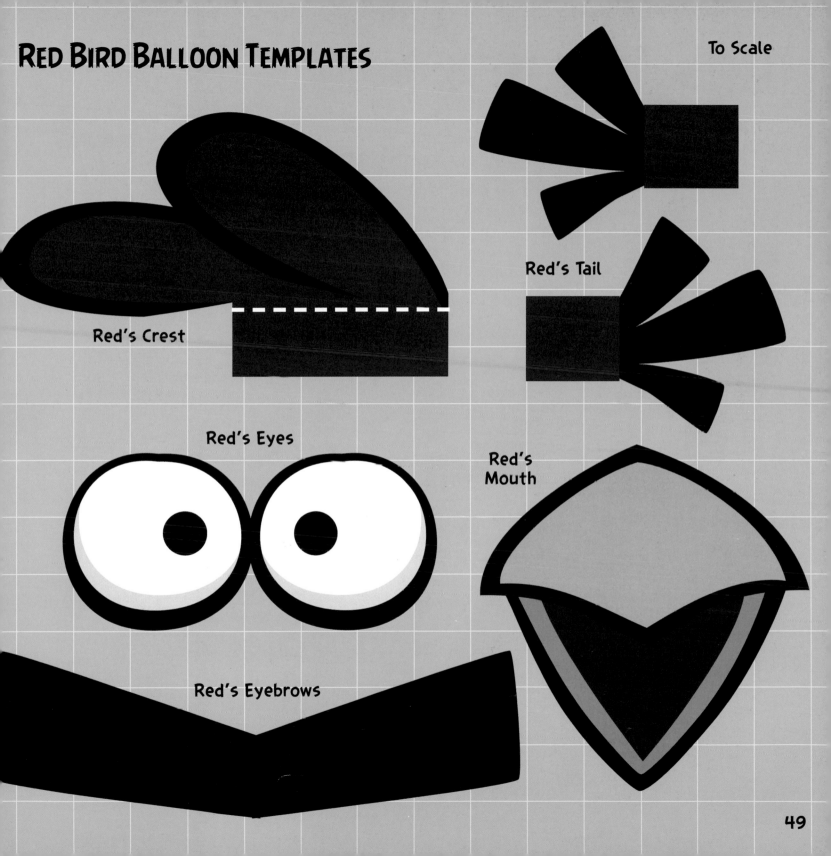

Red Bird Balloon Templates

To Scale

Red's Tail

Red's Crest

Red's Eyes

Red's Mouth

Red's Eyebrows

RED BIRD'S SLINGSHOT

Create this super slingshot to propel your Angry Birds into action!

You will need:

- A ping pong ball
- Paints and paintbrush or felt-tip pens
- A black marker pen
- A piece of fabric 6 cm x 10 cm (2 ½ in. x 4 in.)
- Scissors
- A piece of elastic 35 cm (13 ¾ in.)
- A Y-shaped stick (Ask an adult to help you cut a branch to size and shape, if required.)

Remember ⚠️

Always use your slingshot in a safe place, away from anything breakable and never aim the slingshot at any other people or animals.

1 Using the image above and on page 50 as a guide, paint or colour in the ping pong ball to look like Red. Use a marker pen to add details.

2 Ask an adult to cut a slit at each end of the fabric and to thread the elastic through the ends. The fabric will support Red prior to launching.

3 Tie the ends of the elastic to the stick, as shown.

4 Place Red onto the piece of fabric, pull the elastic back and prepare to launch!

MINION MOUNTAIN

With the help of Foreman Pig, these Bad Piggies have built a structure to help them with their mission to steal the eggs! See how many you can knock down with Red Bird's Slingshot (pages 50-51).

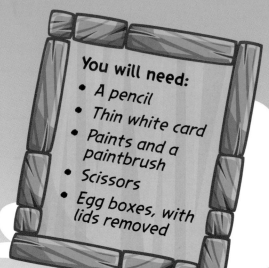

You will need:
- A pencil
- Thin white card
- Paints and a paintbrush
- Scissors
- Egg boxes, with lids removed

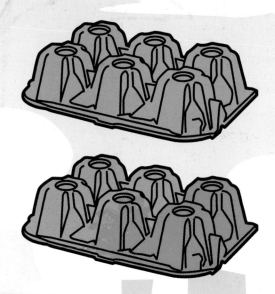

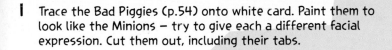

1 Trace the Bad Piggies (p.54) onto white card. Paint them to look like the Minions – try to give each a different facial expression. Cut them out, including their tabs.

2 Turn the egg boxes upside down and paint them in a colour of your choice.

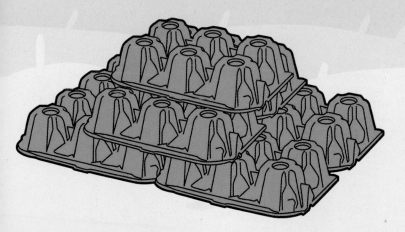

3 Build an egg box mountain by stacking the egg boxes upside down on top of one another, as shown.

4 Fold back the white tabs at the bottom of each Minion and balance them on the mountain. You are now ready to play!

MINION MOUNTAIN TEMPLATES

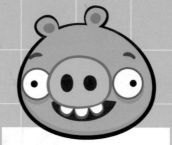

ANGRY BIRDS' MASKS

Will you choose Chuck or Foreman Pig?
Why not make both and give one to a friend!

You will need:

- White card
- Paints and a paintbrush
- A black pen
- Scissors or a craft knife
- Elastic

1 Trace the masks (pp.56-57) onto white card. Paint and draw the features onto each face and leave to dry.

2 Ask an adult to cut out the masks. They will also need to make holes for the eyes and elastic, as marked.

3 Thread the elastic through the holes and adjust the length to fit around your head. Then tie a knot at both ends to secure.

Foreman Pig Mask

To Scale

Chuck Mask

57

ANGRY BIRDS' SCENERY

Create your own Angry Birds drama with this mini theatre. Position the scenery in front of the backdrop, as shown below, and it's time for curtain up!

You will need:
- Thick white card
- Paints and a paintbrush
- Scissors
- Strong white glue
- Long wooden sticks, such as chopsticks or kebab skewers with the sharp points cut off
- Sticky tape

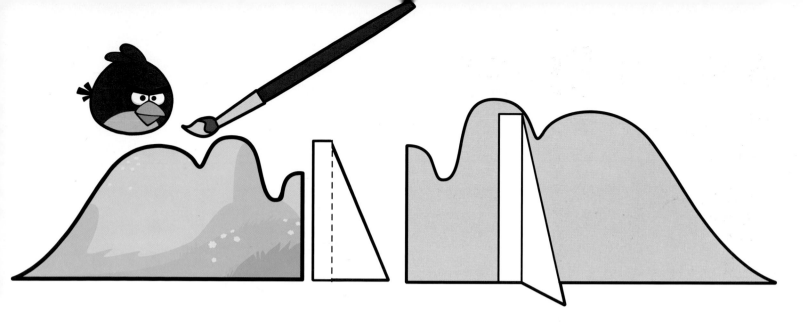

1 Trace the scenery pieces (p.64), backdrop (pp.62-63) and characters (pp.60-61) onto white card. Paint on the details, leave to dry and then cut them out.

2 Fold the two white scenery supports along the dotted lines indicated. Apply glue to the tabs and stick them to the two pieces of scenery so that they stand up.

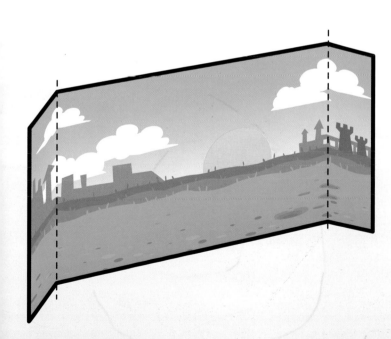

3 Fold the backdrop along the dotted lines, as shown above, so that it stands up.

4 Attach each of the characters to a stick using sticky tape, as shown. Then set up your scenery and start your Angry Birds' show!

Angry Birds' Scenery Templates

Red

Minion Pig

The Blues

Foreman Pig

Matilda

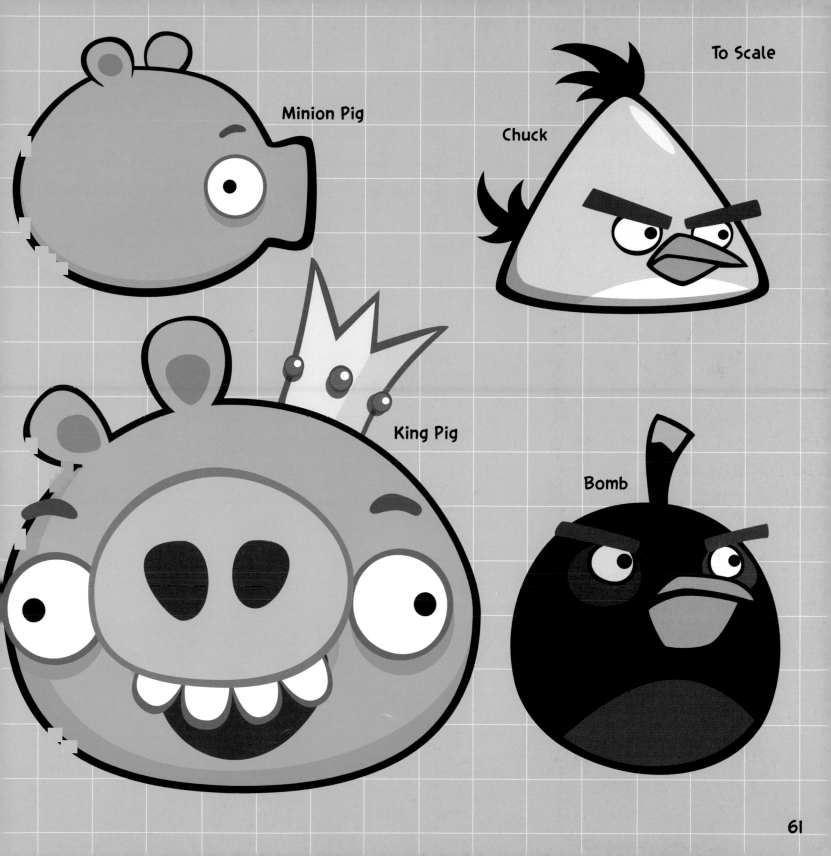

Minion Pig

Chuck

To Scale

King Pig

Bomb

61

Backdrop

To Scale

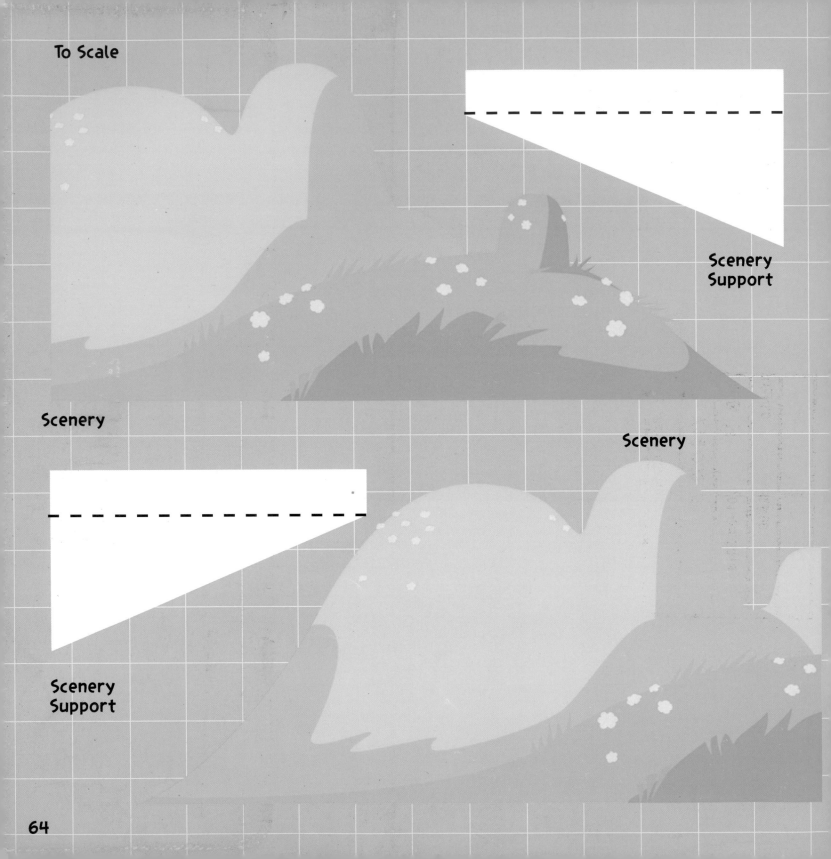

To Scale

Scenery Support

Scenery

Scenery

Scenery Support